History of Britain

Queen Victoria

Andrew Langley

Illustrated by James Field

Heinemann

HISTORY OF BRITAIN – QUEEN VICTORIA
was produced for Hamlyn Children's Books
by Lionheart Books, London

Editor: Lionel Bender
Designer: Ben White
Editorial Assistant: Madeleine Samuel
Picture Researcher: Jennie Karrach
Media Conversion and Typesetting:
  Peter MacDonald

Educational Consultant: Jane Shuter
Editorial Advisors: Andrew Farrow, Paul Shuter

Production Controller: Christine Campbell
Editorial Director: David Riley

First published in Great Britain in 1995
by Hamlyn Children's Books,
an imprint of Reed International Books,
Michelin House, 81 Fulham Road, London SW3 6RB,
and Auckland, Melbourne, Singapore and Toronto.

Copyright © 1995 Reed International Books Limited

ISBN 0 600 58615 4 Hb
ISBN 0 600 58622 7 Pb

British Library Cataloguing-in-Publication Data.
A catalogue record for this book is available
from the British Library.

Printed in Hong Kong

Acknowledgements
All illustrations by James Field except maps, by Hayward Art
Group.
Picture credits
BAL = The Bridgeman Art Library, London., NPG = By courtesy
of the National Portrait Gallery, London, MC = The Mansell
Collection,
RC = The Royal Collection Enterprises Limited/© 1995 Her
Majesty the Queen. RA = Royal Archives, Windsor Castle. MEPL =
Mary Evans Photo Library.
l = left, r = right, t = top, b = bottom, c = centre.
Pages: 4tl: Museum of London. 4br: RC/RA. 5t: RC/RA. 5b:
Weidenfeld and Nicolson Archives. 6bl: MEPL. 6tr: BAL/Forbes
Magazine Collection, New York. 7tl: Weidenfeld and Nicolson
Archive. 7cr: BAL/Guildhall Art Gallery, Corporation of London.
7bl: Gunnersbury Park Museum. 8l: *Punch* magazine/Link House
Magazines Ltd. 8bc: e.t.archive/Stoke Museum/Staffs Poly. 8-9t:
MC. 9r: BAL/Courtesy of the Board of Trustees of the Victoria
and Albert Museum, London.10: RC/RA. 11tl: RC. 11tr: RC/RA.
11c: BAL/Museum of British Transport. 12: RC. 13t, 13c:
RC.13b: MEPL. 14tl, 14tr: Courtesy of the Board of Trustees of
the Victoria and Albert Museum, London. 14b: © Range/The
Bettmann Archive. 14t: BAL/Guildhall Art Gallery, Corporation of
London. 16b: The Royal Photographic Society, Bath. 16tr:
Christie's Images/Gordon Highlanders. 17tl: © The Trustee of the
Wellcome Trust, London. 17cr: MC. 17br: RC/RA.18bl: MC. 18tr:
19bc: MEPL. 19bl, 19 tr: MC. 20tl: MC. 20tr: NPG. 20br:
e.t.archive. 21tr, 21br: MC. 22c: MC. 22tr: CEPHAS/Nigel Blythe.
22br: RC/RA.
Cover: Artwork by John James. Photos: (Albert Hall) BAL/John
Bethell, (Great Exhibition Hall interior) BAL/Stapleton Collection,
(Pot lid showing Victoria, Napoleon II and the Sultan of Turkey)
BAL/Fitzwilliam Museum, University of Cambridge, (Victoria's card
showing dog) RA, (Stamp) Lionheart Books Archive.

PLACES TO VISIT

Here are some museums and sites connected with Queen
Victoria you can visit. There are also parks and memorials to
Victoria and Albert in many parts of Britain. Your local Tourist
Office will be able to tell you about places in your area.

The Argory, County Tyrone, Northern Ireland. Victorian house
with a fascinating collection of furniture.

Balmoral Castle, Aberdeenshire. A small part of Victoria's
favourite home can be seen, with displays of carriages and
royal travels.

Buckingham Palace, London. Many of the main palace
rooms are open, including the Throne Room.

Calke Abbey, Derby. Scarcely changed since the last
century, it is full of everyday Victorian objects.

Castle Museum, York. Includes a reconstruction of a
Victorian parlour.

Fox Talbot Museum, Lacock, Wiltshire. A museum of
photography, in honour of one of its inventors, with many
Victorian images.

Hughenden Manor, High Wycombe. Disraeli's home for 30
years. It was once visited by Victoria.

Kensington Palace, London. Victoria's birthplace. Among
many exhibits is the cot used by all of her children.

Museum of Childhood, Edinburgh. Many Victorian toys and
games.

Museum of English Rural Life, Reading. Many photographs
and tools of the Victorian countryside.

National Railway Museum, York. Includes the queen's royal
train.

North of England Open Air Museum, Beamish, County
Durham. Among the many reconstructions are a Victorian
school room and miner's cottage.

Osborne House, Isle of Wight. The private apartments have
been left exactly as they were when Victoria died in 1901.

Royal Albert Hall, London. An immense round concert hall
built in 1867-71. It was planned by Prince Albert.

Royal Museum of Scotland. The main hall is based on the
design for the Crystal Palace.

Sandringham House, Norfolk. The estate where Prince
Albert Edward went to get away from his mother, though she
did visit here.

Victoria and Albert Museum, London. One of the grand
museums planned by Prince Albert near Hyde Park.

Welsh Folk Museum, St. Fagins, Cardiff. A working
Victorian mill, school and houses with rooms and furniture
from 1800-1900.

Windsor Castle, Berkshire. Visitors can see state rooms,
chapels and the art gallery.

INTRODUCTION

In 1819, the British monarchy was unpopular. George III had been king for a long time, but was now old and blind, and suffered many fits of madness. His eldest son, the Prince Regent, would be the next king. But he was greedy and lazy, and disliked by the British people.

Worse still, the king's sons and daughters were all middle-aged and none of them had any legitimate children. Who was going to inherit the throne after them? Also, this was a time of unrest in Europe. The French had weakened the power of their monarchy in a revolution. Without a future heir, the British monarchy was in danger. At last, on 24 May, the Duke of Kent (George's fourth son) had a daughter, Victoria. One day, she would be Queen Victoria.

CONTENTS

LIFE AS A PRINCESS

Victoria had a lonely childhood. She wrote later that she "had no brothers or sisters to live with – never had a father, and did not know what a happy home life was." Her father died in 1820, when she was a baby. She grew up with her German mother, the Duchess of Kent, in Kensington Palace in London.

◁ **Some of Victoria's dolls.** She had over 100 of them. They were her favourite toys, and she played with them until she was 14 years old.

▽ **Princess Victoria at the age of two with her mother.** She was a bright and lively little girl, but very quick to lose her temper.

Although the Palace was grand, it was a dull place for a child. Victoria was brought up simply and strictly. She did not even have her own room. Afternoon tea was only allowed as a great treat. Her closest friend was her German governess, the Baroness Lehzen.

Because she would be queen, little Victoria was looked after very carefully. She was not allowed to go up or down stairs without holding someone's hand, in case she fell. At the age of eight, she began a daily routine of lessons that lasted from 9.30 in the morning until 6.00 in the evening. First came two hours of geography, history or maths, followed by walking and play. After lunch, she studied languages and religion. She was also taught drawing, music and dancing.

It was not until 1830 that Victoria found out she was heir to the throne. She said immediately, "I will be good!" At that time, her uncle, George IV, was king. He died soon after and was followed by another uncle, William IV. But William was already over 60 years old, and would not reign for long.

Victoria's mother thought the British people should now see their next queen. Between 1832 and 1835, she took Victoria on a series of coach journeys around the country . They visited Wales, the Midlands, the North and East Anglia. The princess was welcomed wherever she went. But back at Kensington Palace, Victoria was unhappy. Her mother and the ambitious Sir John Conroy controlled her every move. The princess hated him, and struggled to resist his clever plotting.

△ **Victoria drew this picture of herself** after she had been ill in 1835.

◁ **The princess with her governess, Lehzen**, and her dog, Dash, at Kensington Palace.

Princess **Victoria !!**

The Inhabitants of
LONDON & WESTMINSTER
Are requested to Close their Warehouses and Shops
On Wednesday, the 24th Inst.
On occasion of Her Royal Highness The
Princess Victoria
Attaining Her Majority.
In Order that all Classes may enjoy a General Holiday on that Happy Occasion.
God Save the King !

[J. HILL, PRINTER, FLEET STREET, LONDON.

△ **A handbill printed in 1837 urging Londoners to celebrate Victoria's 18th birthday.** Victoria was now an adult. The king named at the bottom of the handbill is William IV, the princess' uncle.

THE QUEEN AND CORONATION

On the morning of 20 June 1837, Victoria was woken by her mother. King William had died in the night. Victoria was now the queen. "I am sure," she wrote, "that very few have more real good will and more real desire to do what is fit and right than I have."

At 11.30, she went alone to meet her Privy Councillors. These were the leading politicians and churchmen in the country. Victoria was only 18, and knew very little about politics or government. Yet she was calm and composed as she read out her speech. Everyone was impressed by her. The Duke of Wellington said, "She not merely filled her chair, she filled the room."

The queen quickly began a new life. She moved out of her old home and into Buckingham Palace so that neither her mother nor Conroy could run her life.

▽ **Workers riot in Wales in 1839.** Queen Victoria's early Parliaments ignored workers' demands for fairer ways of electing Members of Parliament (MPs). This led to riots.

◁ **The young queen out riding with her beloved Lord Melbourne** (on the left). On the right is Lord John Russell. Melbourne was Prime Minister until 1841, when he resigned and fell ill. Russell became leader of the Whigs after him, and was later Prime Minister. Victoria never liked him.

◁ **Victoria's coronation in Westminster Abbey in June 1838.** The Archbishop of Canterbury placed the crown on her head. (Inset) A portrait of the new queen in her royal robes.

▷ **As new queen, Victoria travelled in the royal coach** to the Guildhall, where she was to dine with the Lord Mayor of London. Victoria was cheered by huge crowds.

For the first time, Victoria could now do what she wanted. She had her own private bedroom. She went to the opera and the ballet more often. She also began horseriding. As she was very short (only 1.5 metres), she realized that being on horseback made her look taller!

The most important person in Victoria's early years as queen was the Whig Prime Minister, Lord Melbourne. He was 58, and a handsome and witty friend. He and the queen spent many hours together each week, when he gave advice and explained how the government worked. Victoria learned much from Melbourne, who was like a father to her.

The first crisis of her reign came in 1839. Melbourne was defeated in Parliament. The new Prime Minister was to be Sir Robert Peel. Victoria disliked Peel, who was a Tory politician. He asked her to replace some of the Whig ladies in her household with Tories as a sign of her support, but Victoria refused. Peel was forced to give up his attempt to form a government. To the queen's delight and great relief, Lord Melbourne remained Prime Minister.

△ **Common coins from the early years of Victoria's reign.** British currency was then pounds (£s), shillings (s) and pence (d). There were 20 shillings in a pound and 12 pence in a shilling. A shilling was equivalent to 5p in modern money.

THE WIFE OF PRINCE ALBERT

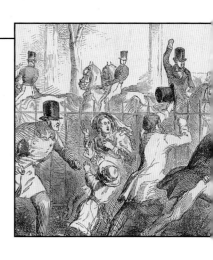

"Albert really is quite charming, and so excessively handsome", wrote Victoria in her journal in October 1839. "My heart is quite going." This was the second time she had met her German cousin, Prince Albert. He was the son of the Duke of Saxe-Coburg-Gotha.

PRINCE ALBERT'S BEE-HIVES.
* These Hives are so constructed, that the HONEY may be removed without DESTROYING THE BEES.—*Morning Paper.*

△ **This cartoon of 1844 of Victoria and Albert** shows their interest in industry and workers.

Some cartoons made only a few years earlier had made fun of the engagement between Victoria and Albert. Because she was queen, it was not right for Albert to propose to her. She had to ask him to marry her. Albert was the son of the Duchess of Kent's brother, and was three months younger than Victoria. But he was much more widely educated. He had been to university and travelled in Italy.

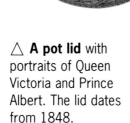

△ **A pot lid** with portraits of Queen Victoria and Prince Albert. The lid dates from 1848.

Albert was good-looking, hard-working and intelligent. He also had a deep interest in the arts and sciences. To the lonely queen, he seemed to be the ideal husband. Victoria and Albert were married in February 1840. She wrote to her uncle, "I do not think it possible for anyone in the world to be happier. He is an Angel." Not everyone agreed with her. Since the time of George I, Britain had been ruled by Germans. Many people disliked the idea of royalty again marrying a German. Parliament refused to give Albert a title, or even a rank in the Army. Londoners sang rude songs about him. But slowly he won the nation's respect.

Married life was difficult for Albert at first. He was unpopular, and had no proper job to do. He spoke English badly, and was very shy. Most difficult of all, his wife was a monarch used to having her own way. Victoria lost her temper very easily, and Albert learned that he had to treat her firmly to keep her calm. Soon, the queen came to depend on her husband. Each day he sat with her at her desk and read through the letters and documents that had arrived. He also began to change the way the Royal Household was run. By cutting out excess, he saved a lot of money.

With Albert, Victoria began to travel more widely. She made her first tour of Scotland in 1841. Two years later, she became the first English monarch to visit France since Henry VIII, some 300 years before. In 1845, Victoria travelled to Germany to see Albert's old home and many of her relations.

△ **An assassin shoots at the queen** as she rides through London with her children in 1849. It was a sign of the unpopularity of the monarchy. Victoria was unhurt. Her courage made her very popular.

▷ **Albert and Victoria are photographed.** The queen was interested in the new art of photography, and had many photographs taken of her family.

△ **Victoria and Albert are shown dancing together** on the cover of this sheet music for a new polka. It was written at about the time of their wedding in 1840. The queen had loved dancing since she was a child, and moved gracefully.

9

FAMILY LIFE

In November 1840, at Windsor Castle, Victoria had her first child, who was named after her. When the doctor told Victoria that it was a Princess, she said, "Never mind, the next one will be a Prince." She was right. Almost exactly a year later, she had a son. He was christened Albert Edward.

◁ (Photo) **The Royal Family at Osborne House on the Isle of Wight in 1857.** It is one of the few photographs to show Victoria and Albert with all their children. The children are (left to right):
● Prince Alfred
● Princess Helena
● Prince Arthur
● Princess Alice
● Queen Victoria with Princess Beatrice
● Princess Victoria
● Princess Louise
● Prince Leopold
● Prince Albert Edward

▷ **Victoria and Albert play hide-and-seek with their young children** in a corridor at Windsor Castle. The queen had had little family life as a child so was delighted to play.

Altogether, Victoria had five daughters and four sons between 1840 and 1857. She did not enjoy having babies. The pregnancies and births caused her great pain, but she felt she had a duty to have lots of heirs to the throne.

The queen and Albert were often so busy that they saw little of the family. They spent the mornings in their separate studies, dealing with state business. There were usually important visitors to entertain at lunch, and several appointments in the afternoon. Dinner was a grand meal, with more guests and members of the court.

However, Victoria and Albert enjoyed relaxing with the family when they were alone. The queen was a strict mother, but loved to watch the Prince playing with the young ones. He would turn somersaults or play games such as blind-man's buff.

△ **Victoria with her daughters Helena and Louise** (on the chair). This photograph was taken in 1852.

◁ (Top) **The Queen and Prince Albert with their five eldest children.** "Bertie", the heir to the throne, stands next to her.

◁ **Princess Vicky and Prince Arthur** dressed in theatrical costumes, in 1854.

Albert took charge of the children's education. Tutors (private teachers) gave them daily lessons in the schoolroom. The Prince himself took them on nature walks. The queen was determined that they should not be spoiled. Their food was simple, and their clothes were handed down to each other. Vicky, the eldest daughter, was very clever. By the age of three, she could speak French, German and English well. But Albert Edward (nicknamed "Bertie") was slow to learn. This worried his parents since he would become king.

ROYAL HOMES

At the start of her reign, Victoria had three royal houses. She did not like any of them. Windsor Castle was "prison-like, large and gloomy," she wrote. Buckingham Palace was cold and full of city fumes. The Royal Pavilion at Brighton was cramped.

▷ **Victoria and Albert travel north to Scotland in the Royal Train** (far right). They sat in their own specially designed carriage. The queen disliked journeys by coach or by sea. (Albert was often seasick.) She found railways comfortable and quick.

▷ **The Royal Family board the Royal Train** for Scotland.

The queen longed for a family home which was private and remote. In 1843, she and Albert visited the Isle of Wight. They liked it, and a year later bought a large estate there called Osborne. Set in a huge park, it had fine views of the sea.

The house itself was much too small for their large family. Albert decided to pull it down and build something grander. He and a builder drew up plans for a new house and gardens. The Prince was involved in everything, including the planting of trees. He took special care to provide proper drains and lavatories. At Buckingham Palace and Windsor, these were smelly and noisy.

The Royal Family moved into their new home only 15 months later, in 1845. Victoria loved Osborne House. She wrote, "How happy we are here!" But her ministers did not like it. If they wanted to discuss important matters with the queen, they had to spend all day travelling from London.

◁ (Top) **Osborne House.** This painting, by Victoria's drawing master, shows the house after it was rebuilt by Prince Albert.

◁ **A picture of Balmoral Castle**, painted in 1853 after it had been extended to suit the Royal Family. Victoria enjoyed the climate here, which was clean and cool. She hated warm rooms, and insisted on having windows open, even in winter.

In 1847, Victoria and Albert bought another house, even further away. They had always greatly enjoyed their trips to Scotland. Now they found a home there, at Balmoral Castle in Deeside. It was a peaceful spot, among hills and woods.

The Royal Family lived a simple life at Balmoral, well away from the usual public attention. They wore tartan kilts, and learned to dance Highland reels. Albert went out fishing and shooting, and began to teach himself the Gaelic language. The queen felt so safe here that she had no troops to guard her, only a single policeman.

△ **A model lodging house**, designed in 1851 by Prince Albert for working people. It was built in Hyde Park in London. Albert was anxious to provide better living conditions for poor people.

THE GREAT EXHIBITION

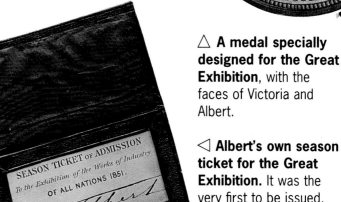

1 May 1851 was one of the proudest days in Victoria's life. Greeted with cheers and music, she entered the new Crystal Palace in Hyde Park. There, she opened the Great Exhibition, a display of industry and inventions. She called it "the most beautiful spectacle ever seen, and the triumph of my beloved Albert."

The Prince had worked hard for over two years to organize this project. The aim of the exhibition was to show off the products of modern science and technology. Albert believed that marvels such as railways and telegraphy would help to make the world more civilized. He also hoped that they would make life easier for poor working people.

The Crystal Palace was itself a marvel. It was designed by architect Joseph Paxton, and looked like a giant greenhouse. Made of iron and glass, it covered an area the size of four football pitches. Many people feared that it would collapse, or that the glass would be shattered by hailstones, but the building stood firm. Inside were nearly 14,000 exhibits (more than half of them British). Some were machines, such as steam hammers, presses and paper-folders. Others were raw materials, such as the enormous Koh-i-noor diamond, and a garden seat carved out of coal. There were also models of new bridges, and a full-size steam locomotive.

The Great Exhibition was a staggering success. During its 140 days, six million visitors came to see it from all over Britain, and from Europe and America.

△ **A medal specially designed for the Great Exhibition**, with the faces of Victoria and Albert.

◁ **Albert's own season ticket for the Great Exhibition.** It was the very first to be issued. The lavatories here were the first public ones in the world.

▷ **Outside the Great Exhibition hall.**

▽ (Below left) **The queen at the Opening Ceremony of the Great Exhibition.** Albert stands with Victoria, next to their eldest children, Vicky and Bertie. In front is the official procession, including the Duke of Wellington and the Archbishop of Canterbury. The Chinese man should not have been there at all. He was a Thames boat owner who was mistaken for the Chinese ambassador!

△ **The Queen and Prince walk down the main avenue of the Great Exhibition.** Victoria often visited the Crystal Palace.

HINDUSTAN

WAR AND DEATH

Prince Albert hoped that the Great Exhibition would help nations to live together in peace. But during the 1850s, wars and revolts broke out in Europe and Asia. British troops fought in several of them. The most important was the Crimean War.

In 1853, Turkey declared war on Russia. The British and French governments decided to support the Turks to prevent Russia expanding its empire. Victoria and Albert were alarmed, and tried to stop the war. Many people were angry at this royal meddling. All the same, British troops were sent to the Crimea, on the Black Sea, in late 1854. They helped to defeat the Russians in an early battle, but the war dragged on for over a year. The Russians made peace in 1856. By that time, thousands of soldiers had died from wounds or disease.

▷ **The Victoria Cross** (VC) was a new medal introduced during the Crimean War. The Queen awarded it to soldiers for heroic deeds in the face of the enemy.

▽ **Photograph of a British horse-artillery camp** in the Crimea. The Crimea is an area of land that juts into the Black Sea.

▷ **Victoria gives medals for bravery** to soldiers wounded in the Crimean War. She invited many injured troops to visit Buckingham Palace.

◁ **The death of Prince Albert at Windsor Castle in 1861**. His doctors believed that he died of the disease typhoid. Only four years earlier, he had been given the title of Prince Consort.

The queen was deeply upset by the hardships suffered by British troops. She presented medals for bravery. She met Florence Nightingale, who set up a nursing service to look after wounded soldiers in the Crimea. She visited military hospitals and urged MPs to improve the conditions there.

Meanwhile, Albert wrote hundreds of letters to ministers, begging them to speed up help for the troops. In fact, his daily routine was beginning to wear him out. Gradually, his health got worse.

In the autumn of 1861, Prince Albert fell ill. He was feverish, and could not eat. Slowly he grew worse, until on 14 December he died. The queen was shattered by the loss. It was the greatest agony of her long life.

▷ **The queen on horseback at Balmoral.** Her servant, John Brown, holds the horse's head. After Albert's death, Victoria relied on Brown's help.

▷ **Albert's tomb at Frogmore in Windsor Park.** Victoria planned to be buried next to the Prince. She ordered sculptures of herself and her husband for the joint tomb. Here Victoria visits the tomb, as she did regularly.

EMPRESS OF INDIA

Victoria was shattered by Albert's death. She spent much of her time far away from London at Balmoral. This made her unpopular, and she was mocked as "the widow of Windsor". It was not until the 1870s that she began to be seen in public again, encouraged by Prime Minister Benjamin Disraeli.

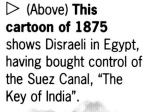

Disraeli flattered and charmed the queen. He also interested her in foreign affairs – especially in the British Empire. This now stretched from Canada in the west, through India and South Africa, to Australia and the Far East. In 1869, the opening of the Suez Canal made the sea voyage between Britain and India much quicker. In 1875, Disraeli bought enough shares in the canal to give Britain control of it. British power in the East grew fast.

Several other nations, including Germany, were also building up their empires overseas. The king of Prussia and the Czar of Russia had both given themselves the title of Emperor. Victoria wanted equal status. In 1876, Parliament agreed to call her Empress of India.

▷ (Above) **This cartoon of 1875** shows Disraeli in Egypt, having bought control of the Suez Canal, "The Key of India".

◁ **A cartoon making fun of the queen becoming Empress of India in 1876**. It shows Disraeli as an Eastern merchant. He is offering Victoria an imperial crown marked India. She is ready to exchange it for her British one. Many people were angry at the queen taking so much power. Over 100 MPs voted against the law making her empress.

"NEW CROWNS FOR OLD ONES!"
(Aladdin adapted)

The queen's new title was announced in India with a grand parade, or durbar. Victoria gave a banquet at Windsor, at which her dress was covered in Indian pearls and diamonds. After this, she always signed herself Victoria RI, meaning Victoria Regina (Latin for queen) and Imperatrix (Empress).

During the 1880s, the empire was expanded even further. Large parts of Africa, as well as Borneo, Burma and New Guinea, came under British control.

▷ **Explorer Henry Stanley greets Christian missionary David Livingstone** in East Africa in 1871. Many Victorian travellers set out to secure new territory for the British Empire, mainly in Africa and the Far East.

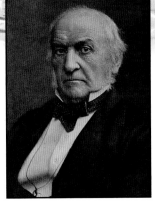

△ **William Ewart Gladstone**, the great rival of Disraeli. He was Liberal Prime Minister four times during Victoria's reign, but the queen never liked him. He tried to prevent the growth of the empire.

△ **A task force of British Navy ships** at Spithead near Portsmouth in 1878. It was assembled to meet the threat of a Russian advance on ports in the Mediterranean. The queen was anxious that the Russians should be stopped. She went to inspect the fleet.

◁ **Victoria visits Disraeli** at his country home, Hughenden Manor in Buckinghamshire, in 1877. The year before she had made him Earl of Beaconsfield.

19

GOLD AND DIAMOND JUBILEES

By 20 June 1887 Victoria had been queen for exactly 50 years. The next day, she drove through London for a Golden Jubilee service in Westminster Abbey. One watcher wrote, "It was one continuous roar of cheering from the moment she appeared!"

△ **The Queen with her daughter, Beatrice**, in 1901.

▷ **Victoria outdoors at work.** She is attended by her Indian secretary.

In front of Victoria rode a grand procession of royal guests from all parts of the world. There were kings and queens from Europe, the Crown Prince of Prussia, the Queen of Hawaii, as well as princes from India, Siam and Japan. Yet, in spite of the celebrations and the cheering crowds, Victoria felt sad. "I sat alone," she wrote, "oh! without my beloved husband!"

She was now more lonely than ever. All of her sons and daughters were married, and most of them had children of their own. They also had powerful positions in Europe. Vicky, the eldest, was wife of the Prussian Crown Prince. Bertie, the heir to the British throne, had married a Danish princess. Others had married into important royal families in Russia and Germany. Alice had died of disease in 1878, and Leopold in 1884.

△ **A souvenir plate commemorating the queen's Golden Jubilee in 1887.** It shows that she had then reigned over a vast empire for 50 years.

VICTORIA
ALL NATIONS SALUTE YOU

△ **Victoria drives through Dublin on a visit to Ireland in 1900.** She had not been there since 1861 because the mayor of the city at that time had refused to erect a statue in memory of Prince Albert.

The Queen was now an old woman. She had grown fat, and despite her shortness weighed nearly 75 kilograms. She suffered from rheumatism and found it hard to walk. Yet she still studied government papers every day. She was at her desk by 7.30 each morning, and sometimes worked until midnight.

There were more celebrations in 1897, when Victoria celebrated her Diamond Jubilee. Another great procession took place, with soldiers from all over the British Empire.

◁ **The queen travels in an open carriage** during her Golden Jubilee celebrations in London in 1887.

▷ **A rare photograph of Queen Victoria smiling**, taken the year after her Diamond Jubilee. She had a good sense of humour, and was remembered for her kindly smile and voice.

DEATH OF A QUEEN

Victoria was 80 in May 1899. Yet she was firm and confident as ever. When British troops suffered a series of disasters against the Boers in South Africa, she was not dismayed. "We are not interested in the possibilities of defeat," she told a minister.

▷ **Victoria with royal relatives from many parts of Europe in 1894.** Vicky is seated on the queen's left, and Vicky's son, Kaiser Wilhelm II of Germany, on her right. Between the Kaiser and the queen stand Nicholas II, the last Czar of Russia, and his fiancée, one of Victoria's granddaughters. Behind the Czar stands Prince Albert Edward (Bertie). He chose to call himself Edward VII instead of Albert.

△ **The monument to Queen Victoria** (seated below the gold figure) outside the entrance to Buckingham Palace as it is today.

▽ **Victoria's funeral procession** on its way through London to Frogmore at Windsor on 2 February 1901.

In July 1900, the queen held a garden party at Buckingham Palace for over 5,000 guests. It was her last big public appearance. She was now tired and weak.

Victoria had begun a journal (diary) as a child in 1832, and kept it faithfully ever since. On 13 January 1901, she dictated her last entry. Nine days later, she died at Osborne House. Her son, Bertie, was now King Edward VII.

The queen's coffin was taken to Portsmouth. Naval ships fired their guns in salute. Then the body was taken to London, where crowds knelt as it passed. Victoria was buried at last in Frogmore, next to Prince Albert.

GLOSSARY

assassin a murderer who sets out to kill an important person.
Boers white Dutch settlers in South Africa.
coronation the ceremony of crowning a king or queen.
empire a number of countries or lands which are ruled by one, often distant, country.
Gaelic the ancient language of Scotland and Ireland.
governess a woman employed to train and teach children in a family.
household people who work for, or live with, the owner of a house.
Liberal one of the two main political parties in Parliament. It grew out of the Whig Party of the early 19th century, and encouraged reform and free trade.
monarch the king or queen. The monarch, as ruler, is said to 'sit on the throne', the official chair, of the country.
Parliament the House of Lords (nobles and important churchmen) and the House of Commons (elected members – MPs) meeting to advise the monarch.
Privy Council a body of ministers and officials who advise the monarch.
telegraph a way of sending messages over long distances by electricity.
Tory one of the two main parties in Parliament, which became the Conservative Party. Most Tories opposed reform and supported the expansion of the Empire.
typhoid a deadly infectious disease caused by germs in food or water.
waltz a dignified ballroom dance, which became popular in the 19th century.
Whigs a political party which opposed the power of the monarchy.

▷ **Victoria's Britain**
This map shows the town and cities mentioned in the book.

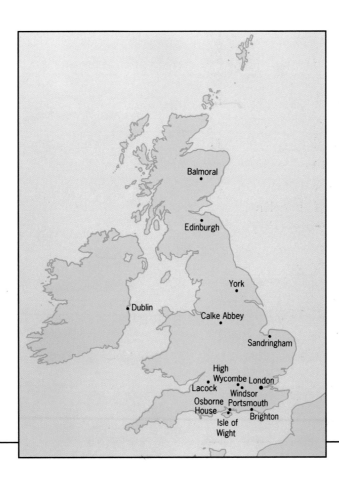

INDEX